LIKE YOU

Cover image: "Rat," oil paint on canvas, by Timothy Rundman

Book design by Rebecca Wolff

Published in the United States by

Fence Books
110 Union Street
Second Floor
Hudson NY 12534

www.fenceportal.org
518-567-7006

This book was printed by Versa Press www.versapress.com
and distributed by Small Press Distribution www.spd.org
and Consortium Book Sales and Distribution www.cbsd.com

Library of Congress Control Number: 2020951956

Roberts, Beth (1965–)
Like You / Beth Roberts

ISBN 13: 978-1-944380-19-9

First Edition
10 9 8 7 6 5 4 3 2

Fence Books are published with the support of all Friends and Members of Fence.

LIKE YOU

beth roberts

THE OTTOLINE PRIZE

Fence Books

HUDSON NY

CONTENTS

Evolvers

Chimera

Putti

Notes

Thanks

EVOLVERS

AT THE PENULTIMATE MOMENT

What could happen next, just before light refolds the corner, runoff pools,
a needle falls and the glint appears to the thought of the biographer
of the mother of the father with the hand in the mind you made up.

Who doesn't want to behold the red button, the murder weapon before it was?
Who doesn't want to have had the weapon before it was used? Who doesn't want?
Who doesn't? Who? Everyone's clever until the error is laid bare and bleeding.

Something happens next, becomes more or less beautiful, finishes coming
and just bes, I mean is. Something lives at the penultimate moment.
At, of, or in the unbutton, it lives with some fibers attached.

IN THE HOLY POLAR VORTEX

In the polar vortex we are all friends. We all are friends, for we are cold and going to be colder, and we warm to each other. After 9/11 we were friendly—actually it was more like our hatred in that thick moment agglomerated, refocused and massed into a thumbprint somewhere, not here. For a time we walked down the dirty and clean streets looking kindly into each other's eyes.

What could happen now if we walked down the street? Going through extreme cold bares us thrillingly. Dressing for the weather is like undressing for others, and undressing for the weather is the wild. If you want to see a fox in the woods across the street, see a red fox. If you want to see your unborn, find them in the clearing and retrieve them from the cold.

GOOGLING EARTH

You roll into sight, Alabama, Alaska, Arizona, Arkansas, California, Colorado, Connecticut, Delaware—we almost forgot about Delaware—Georgia, Mount Narodnaya, Sverdlosvsk Oblast, Tomsk Oblast, Novosibirsk Oblast, Koryak Mountain range approaching the Arctic softspot.

We would rather raise you in our homeland of triple shorelines, perhaps on the reservation. The place you would think of in the future, when you hear certain music. We would raise you somewhere safe, if only you were ours. If you were only ours. Instead, we just can't take

our eyes off you crawling down the street where we live, babbling, a little blue, figuring it out. Eventually you will reach the intersection. And because you really are the one we've always wanted, we'll hold you there a minute, and marvel at you a while, as we consider where to go next.

THE LAND OF REASON

This life-of-our-gorgeous-planet video series goes for the wide shot
using the perspective of a high drone or giant bird floating latitudinally,

which on land would suffocate admirers with its bulging feathers, lacking feet.
One far image circumvents the big picture, being only a beautiful abstract

quaint as a quilt compared to farmland, or farmland to an engraving,
though in fact it is tributaries after a Monsoon rain,

a place where baboons select a path through shallows to their usual spot,
now highly strange. Their expressions say *it all*.

Viewers absorb the main points, admire the intagliated landscape, or wait
for more baboons. But maybe you see the footprints.

THEY WHO MAKE THE QUIET QUIETER

An owl stroked the midair of the ravine, making the quiet noon quieter.
A mountain stood before the stars and stopped their ears, their quiet calls.

A president, reading to a classroom, understood horror as a different word.
A zealot told the chosen where they stood, understanding a different cold.

A parent died and left a child with a memory of their language.
A phone called, buzzed, then vibrated, making the quiet room quieter.

An extremely rare animal disappeared in the blunt landscape of media channels.
We don't know yet what it was, perhaps a salamander.

SPOTTED DEER

What do you call it when you drove with your dad out to the forties so he could see if you could see deer, and you balanced coffee in teacups while the truck picked up ruts and put them back down,

because the forties were his and he knew every doomed jack pine, red pine, red anthill, badger hole, blueberry bush, silver birch, back switch, backdrop, dropped antler, deer blind,

because he wanted it for you, which you saw from the window and sprung seat as you spotted deer, but never loved enough till now—his reformed ashes

bits akin to bone, lying amid lichen in the rye patch he'd planted to draw the herd, hold them in his sight, though oft distracted by the sunset on their fur and in the air?

ON IMPACT

We're going to die and nobody can tell us what's that like, let alone put it to music, which is about a stellar autopsy,

what astrophysicists do, not to determine cause of death but a former star's continuing influence. One put it to music:

as the star became a nebula certain parts were the bass and the harps (harps!), then flutes, of course the cymbals crashed.

It's not what I'd choose, but still, so damn dear we assign it to science and make sure we all hear it.

What I really want to know is how we'll manage the hallelujah that'll feed the black hole.

Who cares we found some footprints in the snow? What about a shrinking borealis? My mother wants to know

why do people even wonder what's out there. I think she's worried you're watching, and finding our fading fascinating.

BACK TO THE VILLA

Sun pressed down and the hill was soothed. All day we turned our backs to the villa, hoping to appear ourselves later.

In the distance, olive groves held inroads lined with the cedars from California, dropping cones and sending incense.

Up close were doves. They transferred light, lavender and rosemary, cooed a brief crush on humility. In the distance a priest

blessed a horse, not the rider. Later the crowd engulfed the angular horse that won alone for heaven or history, or both.

By evening the moon promised only good fat. Swallows and boars approached the swimming pool very differently.

Fireflies were slower. They created fine blue dashes against the dark, a patient and fundamental code. They are slower.

THE WAGER

If I could choose between calling back to being my father's father Earl and mother's mother Hilda, the last two people I knew with a wager,

or seeing my father suddenly round the corner in that paradoxical glow rounding the corners, then I choose the one person.

If I have to choose between him and something else, I don't want him back, not much older than I, inured too long and wavering.

I don't choose solid ground for architects, a fair atmosphere, the return of a government or species. I want to change the moment my lover's mind changed,

a minor evolution in this massive dream we made you make, yet I swing from branch to branch to get you back before I wake.

ONE WAY

First we must drive the truck across the river up the highway to an exit through
a tripping town and out again along

A narrowing road turning gravel through the hot hills and cooling ditches,
no radio on, no hard on, no buzz on,

Take an offshoot into a field that seems to hold everything we knew and trample
those details with our triple treads,

Continue to the edge of a hollow like the dip at the base of your neck where a pulse
lives below my fingerprint,

Leave the truck to descend in sun a soft path to a faint crack, a creek whose surface
magnetizes the miniscule hairs on our presence, so

We can never again leave that place or change into other versions like woolly bears
hideous in the headlights

NOSTALGIA

What if Rockwell did paint a man and woman entering the cornfield with that look
between them?

They would not be barefoot, since they understand about cornfields. But their shoes
might look like

they are not worn as much as they could be. For once, the sky is not beatific.
Blue, of course,

but dark at the clouds' edges, for all our sakes. What does happen in the rows?
They kneel, he first,

so she must bend slightly more than the stalks; then she, so his head is in the clouds.
Then he turns her

toward the field's floor, where the smooth, green and maroon roots raise themselves
above the soil surface,

which is what the plant needs to grow to 9 feet and all ears tipped with shredded silk,
almost too much to bear.

WHITE-THROATED SPARROWS, BOY SOPRANOS

In the future, the vampires will ask: Why did you love us so much in the 21st century?

And we will reply: We saw ourselves in reflective skin and lost ourselves in thirst.

It wasn't soullessness, they'd say. A morality made you want to exchange the planet for gods.

It was poetry, we'd try. A way to fill ourselves. Sex, heavy metals, war machines, the blood of the world ...

Yes, they would pronounce through their teeth: Give us your list again. Try to explain.

And we: We had wet throats and curved wings, but could not fly and sing.

SOBER

Walk into the bedroom, put new sheets on the bed, and pillowcases.
Walk out the house into daylight, turn up the alley, notice rutabagas.

Don't know what they are.
Know enough, though.

Notice the clouds above your head, and they nod so slowly:
clouds over the bridge building like marble headstones.

There are flowers all over, they don't seem to matter much.
There is always greenery, everywhere yearning past hunger.

Hunger shaped like a hanger, or a hunter.
Eat dull food after preparing it with sharp knives.

Dull is plodding from place to place, placing yourself.
Put yourself into a wanted sign, a kind of distraction.

Use the garden, that's what it's for.
Listen to song, that's what it's for.

Hear how songs make edges finer.
It's what you wanted.

Things with edges make corners and borders on time.
They are there to remind you you should feel hurt:

trains, cicadas, near riots, parents, signs for prisoner of war–missing in action, wanter, signs for this place is for sale, writing on the walk, empty cans, waking hour, want, can't.

ROUGH HOUSING

The earth houses water molecules older than it, water broken during an early moment
and resurfaced in the ocean encompassing all current and late creatures,

and those bodies landed in us, made as well of water and a variety of additional atoms.
But I found a small, barely pliable snake in the cellar,

brought it out to damp ground near the first of the green, and there was no recognition.
A white butterfly appeared peripherally, a lot of light for such a dry being.

Things that defy gravity are surpassed only by things that were beneath the snow, such as a chicken hat found beside an opened bag of marshmallows. Also a chicken hat defies gravity in either case:

whether a hat for a chicken or a hat like a chicken, the latter generally being for a child, which defies gravity. It might be said these things usurp, rather than surpass, those things that defy gravity.

Also, defiance might be described as "flying in the face of," such as "a chicken hat flew in the face of gravity." Many other things fly in the face of, or are found beneath, gravity and snow, respectively:

any steam, one child's rain, flames, architecture, thieves on crosses, agriculture, a horse galloping, a horse plasticized, 90-degree angles, angels right and wrong, bread, fresh marshmallows, news, song.

A PAIR OF AIRS

For Summer, from Winter

A little bird said
you're thinking of me.
I get wild with torture,
poor chickadee.

Should I warm to a halo
or an angel in the snow?
Summertime, I'm afraid
I don't remember how.

Here is a snowflake
that looks like a lover
swaying in shallows
by the cliff he went over.

For Winter, from Summer

My days are so long, Jack.
I'll meet anywhere you name.
Meet me in the longest shadow,
I won't tell anyone you came.

I look for you in dark looks
where crystal eyes could be.
I look for you where love left
and leaves follow me.

I received your snowflake!
It looks like clover turning
in complicated, implicated,
icy rapids, and I'm burning.

2-STEP ROUND AND REEL

I like how you look
I like how you fuck

I like how you smell
I like how you smile

How you fuck like you look
How you smell like you smile, you

Look
Like you

How you
Like I

JUST AS LONG AS SPACE IS

You see, a billion years later, the gravitational wave of two black holes powered like a billion-trillion suns,

just as we can sometimes be and-or are somewhere, wove through space-time, our context, *our* meaning

little us who are tiny we smally producing production and destroying destruction here where-when, and

while you completely slept in see-through moonlit pajamas out to your utmost periphery, chirped.

THE WORK OF THY HANDS

I asked Quan if there was a Western equivalent to the message or symbol portrayed by beheading.
He said not really.

Not a lynching?
But he had moved on to the clean flash of a Japanese sword, a thing of beauty and no comparison.

I had pictured a body kneeling still, still with a dream at the head.
The enemy swelling or desiccated beside

the body suspended and relocating itself briefly between ground and air, then a thought flying out.
But that is not it.

This changes everything. I learned the usual way is to hack through the neck.
Saw a way out.

How much time from beginning to end depends on the persons. How much pain changes cannot
be determined, even on video, but the persons do not

anticipate a quick breach and then light. They have time to look at the hard work of their hands,
veins leading over the knuckles, ways out of the wilderness.

FOR ALL THINGS NOW LIVING

For the painter whose sky keeps changing, for the sky that covers and wounds us with astonishing
light, for those who choose wisely for us, for scientists who say the sky will wound us with
astonishing light, for things we can see for ourselves, things whipping sideways as we stand still,
flags and vines ripped free, generations of insects and rockets, and Zeno's arrow singing,

for things that stay as we flash by, fields and woods and ruins and tales, breath-like citizens
reflecting their place, what stands for our ever, things surrounding, within or without us
so we are engulfed, engorged, endangered or ignored, things that take over, joy, for deep
and shallow offices, for things that turn our heads, for the stuttering dread that almost

stops us, flashes of pity, the horse that looked through white eyelashes, for things we set by
on the shelf, things that change us when we want more of the same, all the blinding selves all
around, all the time, for communities of the molecular and policies of the muscular,
for the progenitors, for things that must look at the sun, for lovers, forever,

for deeply old children who never looked to forget, but, distracted by changing, did lose sight
of their grand canyon and hymnals and errors and tools and blood debt and vision and all
the beauty of our trembling day-lit backyard, our routine and adored, astonishing memory,
our reach and our least or last notice.

THE BRIGHT SIDE

Take another shot at me, the rain is puncturing everything and the weather does the rest. And then the weather makes up for it all. No matter how many times you plant my fingernails to grow a new devil,

I will always see a reflection on the hard surface, always break my distrust against the edges, claim the superficial like a slow child on the wrong path. On the way are more open spaces. On the way has always been

our story with its tragedies like blunt civilizations and tragedies like small toads. On it goes. More than anything I want to feel the sun like a body I'll never have to leave, and therefore conspire against nothing.

CLEAVE

Heart got lost and moved into the brain.

There it displaced some of the same old thoughts,
but the ones that remained didn't say to get lost again.

At the first sudden heartbreaking realization,
the same old thoughts said, what were you thinking?

But all the heart heard was you thinking.

CHIMERA

LOUD

I began after an unusual look at the research showed you that
A human animal in you could put an animal human in me. Or

The human in you brought out the animal in me. Roar.
The human in you put out the animal in me, put it out like a cat.

You were supposed to have an extra set of eyes on you, but you
Can't handle but one true thing at a time. Let me in. Roar.

You wake up thinking there's something the data isn't telling you.
There is something the data isn't telling you. Everything is true.

THIS IS NOT A POEM

This is a memory.

This is the church, this is the steeple, open the doors: where's all the people?
This is the church, this is the steeple, open the doors: there's all the people.

This is not a poem.

The shepherd carried the lamb all the way to the shoreline and made it a fisher of men.
The ethics committee approved fishing up to 28 days for the quicksilver embryos.

This is a policy.

Humans might go places within the animal's body they aren't intended to travel.
Therefore animals' bodies must be restricted in certain places, such as the hippocampus.

This is not a poem.

The body is a temple worn down by lenders too big to fail, so while the music distracts
you search for a way in, and you search for a way out, and all the while the organ plays.

This is a truth.

"It might be possible to 'generate an unlimited supply of therapeutic replacement organs.'"
"So far, about 20 pig-human or [and?] sheep-human chimeric embryos have been created in the project,

This is a project.

"but the researchers did not bring any of those embryos to term."
This is a project like every project because of the endgame: there's all the people.

This is a sort of map.

You shall circumvent other primates lest the chimera resemble and love and/or hate you and the meek inherit the map once the moratorium is lifted.

LIKE A PERSON

I am sated constantly.
I stay at the water's edge all day, never remonstrated,
never chased away.

Metaphor, I took to it like a person.
I don't know what's better, metaphor or water.
Water is everywhere and metaphor

nowhere but never as gone as water.
Like you I can't help putting words together, can't help
putting my mouth to water.

I take to it like an animal. Like yours
my mouth waters like sea level describing a shoreline
when I can't help it.

"DESCRIBE YOURSELF USING THREE WORDS"

Even when the world did not need another person and you did not need another person, you made one.

And when that one sickened you fixed it. And when it got sick again you fixed it again.

And when it called to you from deep inside the labyrinth you turned inside out so it could find its way

and when it died anyway, you hated and loved more, no zero, all surplus. I am here
I answer, I answer you.

I MAKE A JOKE

What I am not: a rat, a rat-mouse, a mouse-rat, a mouse, a man-mouse, a woman at home.
None of these comes close.

My first place was not a womb, but neither was yours necessarily. You see, like you,
I know more than you know and less than you think.

I make a joke. What do you get when you cross what with whom? Atom.

Like yours, my skin is an organ and my heart a mobile device.
Someday it will send me a message through static, and I will make myself a nest of trouble.

What I am: at home. What I am: homespun. What I am: offspring. What I am: like you.
Like you: proportional to everything.

"DO YOU HAVE ANY QUESTIONS?"

How do you watch people take another person down, take a person away?
Do you lack sufficient data? Is it a kind of defiance?

If defiance, does the person on the ground know it?

But if the person lacks sufficient data, what good could come of it?
If you stare at this overflow, do you see too much or too little, and

if the person on the ground sees you looking hard at their sake, at gaps
between blows, isn't that largesse of absence?

But if instead you scream and then two or more of you scream at them to stop?
Would that be sufficient data to give them back to their life.

If you yourself are two or more, in fact in one, but seeing with two eyes—
one on a rib cage, one a child's morning in the sun—could that overwhelm?

Would the person know or feel that, being led away? Being dragged?

LIARS POETICA

You mean to live for a very long time as I am meant to go on forever.

My kind leaves by medevac as your kind lives in the house of the lord forever.

Your kind votes in asymptotes that it will dwell in the house of the lord forever.

We share so much difference we are as divisible as waves from sea or sound.

And when your lies roar and roar, roar and roar all night I lick my wound.

IN POSSIBLE

And how is it possible you don't protect your babies?—
that you stand alongside and watch for a time and even look away

while the young are not snatched up and torn into, but in fact are
taken apart slowly by what you don't do to protect them?

I do know. You hate your species but are distracted by love of survival,
a long losing. And your young grow terrible in the world you made

and when you feel yourself enemy, you only wait—suddenly enemy
you make your fear fashion and lie in wait.

Someday you will tell your babies a story of me to distract them:
How I grew up alongside a wall, a protection.

IN THESE PARTS YOU CREATED WORRISOME PLACES

In these parts you created worrisome places nevertheless dear to me and to you,
capable of drawing another
to me, generative.

I know there are two sides to my sexual nature, as in the world there are actors—
populations of cons, of pros, makers and fakers
like you and me,

and also the pluripotential for the act—explosion, immolation, general fire and war.
And also the existence of rare
forms of recourse.

The place you had to go for me was dark, so dark the blast you made blew it apart.
Violent but not all wrong.
It's all right.

WITH HER

One day at sea level I taught a child to categorize. We started with her animals.
Animals of the jungle, in the trees, on the savanna, on the farm, on three or four legs, mystical.
Or as she said, mythical.

Then we started arranging the animals around us. Animals below, on, and above the sand.
Sand crabs and shifting exoskeletons, stars, birds, then birds and stars.
She told me she already knew people are animals.

We separated the people into different kinds of animals.
Animals of the city, in the desert, on the farm, friends, strangers who may be friends but maybe
not, elves, teachers, police officers, lab coats, mommies and daddies.

She said she sold seashells by the seashore.
She said she knew what kind of animal I was and then what other kind of animal I was. I was
a stranger friend on three or four legs. The tide was coming in.

MOVEMENT

You are concerned about a lack of moral clarity.
It made its way along the tracks and mountain paths,

up out of kitchens in the ditches of those towns
and into the big white house.

I am never surprised you are often surprised.
To stay in place you eat your young; others look on.

But in a memory or dream we have,
our flock or pack or pod is devotional and moving.

LIKE A BURNING UNDERSTORY

It is hot in Florida, where 125 wildfires burn today and 2,000 since January.
The sand doesn't actually burn so you go there.

I know about pseudospeciation, an entire population called the enemy.
My other species leaves danger behind and not the baby.

I mean a whole population is the enemy, not calls the enemy.
I think you must think a forest goes deeper and deeper

and deep inside, your laws and rules apply either not at all or perfectly.
It's all the same in Florida, burning equally unevenly.

It will all become clear when we break for the spires and tall grass together.
An entire population called the enemy.

A SONG FOR SOME CHILDREN

You and I are alike as a desert and a dust bowl,
as an air raid and tornado sound the same siren.

Do you sing I can save you from your future?

A man walks a dog as the sky grows fur,
the sky unethical, the dog good, a cat following.

Can I still save you for the future, do you sing?

The sky goes black and white so the animals run
back to the horizon where we all start again.

FAQS

(You didn't know not to remove the bee from the flower.)
When bees are close to death, often they cling to flowers.

It died after you touched it softly aside with your pen
but it wasn't because of you and your pen.

(O but it was, and its death was
and by your standards writ large, is.)

‡

Your artifice made me real.
Your artifice made me realize

Any style of life
Is prim

Christian was thinking of primroses touched softly aside
to make the microbe respond in protein

The faerie is rosy
Of glow

‡

What is "more than human"? I have not done all the reading. What I understand is that when humans, realizing the power to lay waste their world, remain as a body comprising only particular humans, all else that has been alive around but not in or of that body is more or less than human.

‡

What is in or of me? I feel myself
anthropocene bling showing
you off, what you're made of.

I like this idea very much, this and that
at that moment he was thinking of
primroses, the faeries inside them.

COUPLET

occasionally
a mating
a joyful snarl

when where
his finger trailed
the hairs rose

"IN ITS ACCLIMATION TO CLIMATE CHANGE, THE CHIMERA SHINES"

I like how you are about the weather:
it snows and you have "snow days" and rain makes you thoughtful and alone.

I see your eyes when the weather changes
belong to better persons altogether, "inside" or "outside," especially in spring, so

I am unsure what will happen when sick bats and frogs start to fall from the sky.
Though I could turn inside out.

"WHAT IS YOUR MOTHER'S MAIDEN NAME?"

In other words you want to know who my mother is, who she was in other words
and in other words
other worlds?

You're the fuckers who grabbed her in the first place and made her something so
thing, so other
than a first place.

You know who she is. Her maiden name is O la la. Her, her maiden, her maiden name,
her maiden name is O
la la.

JUST A MOMENT

You are one of the organisms who notices the moon no matter the stage, but leaning toward
the full or waning crescent more than the waxing gibbous,

so you think you do not want the scientifically or poetically strenuous responsibility of the actual
pig-human on your hands. Only you do want it in your hands

for just a moment until your better angel gets the best of you, and until then
you will see it looks like a turning into a knot, like the one we're in now, uttering something

to humans and non-humans and more-than-humans, all resembling their ancestors, some
the chimeras known as angels, others others, and you will never forget its light.

IT'S BEEN REAL

It's been 90 million years since I had only one ancestor, and 90 million since you shared one.

Now

you pulled me into a new scene, in which my vocabulary improves fast enough to never quite

capture the moment

that never is allowed. Never made you make clones and drones and ibones, and never shall

twain meet

so here I am, another one among the populations considered to be not as quite as implicated

in the anthropocene,

the women and the poor, and the other more-than-animals, though I admit I represent the gall

that got you here

I mean got us here, got us all here shifting in our populations of cells who are nothing if not

bright-eyed.

OF SPRING

Under the sun I am like you. I witness lilacs on their stems and don't know what to do.

If I could be both at once I might hear flowers speak instead of inflating heads of seeds and words,

and if I could escape the defining aspects of my model and focus on what we see in this same sunshine,

I might describe other warmth to you, how I outlived a virus by generations, making me a better animal

and someone with whom you could feel at home caring less for the language of flowers.

OF NATURE'S PEOPLE

People do escape into the woods.
They hide in the trees, they shoot

into a cold bared wind,
at animals at all levels

including themselves.
In the future we will turn to wilderness,

not having been there in the first place
or else returning, redacted

by the internecine or
loosened by the hurricane.

I know some of nature's people.
If you were to come with me

into the field, a yellow field
lined with woods without hesitation

our several natures might meet
in the yellowing.

PUTTI

Between the turning blades of turbines is the shape of something coming, made by the space between electricity and wind, so

the sockets of Jeff's Market in Wilton and West Liberty glow in their plots at the end of the first short streets cradling a kinesthesia

particular to winter nights only in America where a great bird can soar so headless across fields until dawn creates and breaks.

FIGHT CLUB AT THE MUSEUM

Its historical backdrop is a prop for smearing their selves against, for their rage,
ground to a point by the constant hours of settling down or failing to stand up.

And so the afternoon is subsumed by a structural takeover as within bare seconds
their cells change and each takes each to another place, like fucking hate

the sunset-colored devils think as they lay each other out on the poured slab.
Heroes stand in the corners and putti float with diminishing motives, while further

in the museum a skull remembers laughter, light as mayflies against a screen.
A quietude made by having lived continues being disturbed by having lived.

SKULL THOUGHT

Music at first when out of the dim room a little light
not light, music
in geometric shards, music motes

gather like a hand lying in church, a hand on
beings with
silky hair over an orb or globe, small words

heads offering something, dot of salt disappearing, and
through the ticking of a seam
thought

places, as a filtered melody in a moment in a giant life also
is momentous,
a memory

ANOTHER MEMENTO

Goers stop at the skull and search its mind:
inverse parabola at the crown housing its only thought,

brow cool for a palm, parietal and temporal,
teeth in a grit—material and portal for their own one thought,

especially those orbits of the eyes, absence where paired
answers swirl, and hollow nose.

SKULL REMEMBERS

Then they warmed each other. Now is like
then, except without any others. Sometimes

words enter the museum windows where light curls.
Sometimes the words gather in memory remains

and make them behave in a way. Then they feel like
a silky umbilical stream. They feel like fingerprints.

They smell like a small damp head.
They smell like pith. They taste like salt.

They look like history upon introduction.
They sound like the last thing the skull said.

LOOK

Sometimes a child in the museum stops and stares.

The skull does nothing but stare.

It's delightful.

Notes

Credit to Jeff Tady for **EVOLVERS**, the title of one of his beautiful drawings.

1 One detail of the painting "The Lacemaker" by Vermeer shows coiled red thread looping out of a pillow and over a table edge. Not yet quite its more material self within the more established world of the painting, the thread still bears the appearance of its essential self, which is paint.

5 When George W. Bush learned of the second passenger plane crashing into the second World Trade Center tower on Sept. 11, 2001, he paused for a moment and then continued reading to the elementary schoolchildren whose classroom he was visiting in Sarasota, Florida.

7 In 2014 I heard a story about graduate student Wanda Diaz-Merced, who was blind and studied astronomy through sound. Diaz-Merced worked with Harvard professor Alicia Soderberg to put to music the deaths of stars, assigning different instruments to each of the signals—radio, x-rays, light. The music for each stellar autopsy is different because every star, and its demise, is different.

17 This is a song for two voices.

18 Another song, this might be sung and danced to the tune of "Mairi's Wedding." Being a round, the "I" at the end rounds back up to the "I" at the beginning.

19 On February 11, 2016, LIGO (Laser Interferometer Gravitational-Wave Observatory) detectors heard the sound of two black holes colliding. The gravitational waves produced a sound that rose to a higher frequency at the end, like a "chirp."

27~42 This and most poems in this section get their life from the work-in-progress of University of California, Davis, research biologist Dr. Pablo Ross (and others around the world) to create chimeric embryos by injecting human stem cells into pig embryos, through which the stem cells might grow into human organs used for biomedical purposes.

28~29 Quotes are from *LiveScience*, "Strange Beasts: Why Human-Animal Chimeras Might Be Coming," Rachel Rettner, August 5, 2016.

33 This was after reading Ilya Kaminsky's poem "The Townspeople Watch Them Take Alfonso Away."

41~42 At the University of Calgary, experimental poet Christian Bök has been engineering a living poem called The Xenotext, stored entirely in bacterium DNA. In the process put very simply, Bök writes a poem in English, then writes code that translates the poem into an alphabetical DNA sequence; a microbe responds by building (or "writing out") a protein, which has a DNA sequence that can then be translated back into English. In this way, given the first line of his sonnet Orpheus, "Any style of life is prim," the bacteria responds with:

The faery is rosy
Of glow

It would be funny to call the work ongoing, as it's likely the bacteria (*d. radiodurans*) will outlive humanity.

45 Credit goes to C. D. Wright and her "in a word, a world" for some of the thinking behind "in other words | other worlds?"

50 The term "nature's people" is from Emily Dickinson and her "A Narrow Fellow in the Grass (1096)."

Thanks

Thank you to Ander Monson, Matt Hart, Matthew Lippman and Joshua Marie Wilkinson, editors of the journals where these poems appeared:

Diagram Skull thought; Another memento; Skull remembers; Look
Forklift, Ohio Spotted deer
Love's Executive Order Liars poetica
The Volta At the penultimate moment

Thank you to Cullen Bailey Burns, Ryan Collins, Alexandra Elias, Jeff Krebs, Farah Marklevits, Nathan McDowell, Tim Rundman, Aubrey Jane Ryan, L. A. Street, Ivan Starenko, Rosalie Starenko, and Jeff Tady, all of whom in various ways helped me make this book.

Deepest thanks to Rebecca Wolff and Fence Books.

The Ottoline Prize is made possible by its sponsor, Jennifer Epstein.

Since 2002, and formerly known as the Alberta Prize and the Motherwell Prize, this award is given to a book of poems written by a person who is a woman and who has published at least one previous full-length collection of poetry. The prize includes a cash award, publication, and a two-week residency at the Eliot House in Gloucester, Massachusetts.

Previous winners of the prize include: Chelsey Minnis, Tina Brown Celona, Sasha Steensen, Rosemary Griggs, Ariana Reines, Laura Sims, Elizabeth Marie Young, Lauren Shufran, Kaisa Ullsvik Miller, Josie Sigler, Harmony Holiday, Stacy Szymaszek, Wendy Xu, Lesle Lewis.

Fence publishes with the support of members, organizations, and institutions. A not-for-profit corporation, Fence is mandated by its board to make decisions in keeping with its mission

TO MAINTAIN A VENUE, IN PRINT, AURAL, AND DIGITAL FORMS, FOR WRITING THAT SPEAKS ACROSS GENRE, SOCIO-CULTURAL NICHES, AND IDEOLOGICAL BOUNDARIES, AS ACCESSIBLY AS POSSIBLE SUCH THAT FENCE PUBLISHES LARGELY FROM ITS UNSOLICITED SUBMISSIONS, AND IS COMMITTED TO THE LITERATURE AND ART OF QUEER WRITERS AND WRITERS OF COLOR. FENCE ENCOURAGES COLLECTIVE APPRECIATION OF VARIOUSNESS BY INHERING COLLECTIVELY OUTSIDE OF THE CONSTRAINTS OF OPINION, TREND, AND MARKET.

Fence welcomes new members. Joining means you receive books, magazine, a tote or other memento, handmade Editor Juice, and connection via landline (518-828-1825).

WE ALSO WELCOME YOUR IDEAS ABOUT WHAT YOU WOULD LIKE FROM FENCE IN EXCHANGE FOR YOUR SUPPORT.

Join online at fenceportal.org/support